When I go fishing I just like to eat candy.
Kara

My Daddy gets so mad when I throw my pole in the water.
Stephen

One time I threw my lure out and it never came back.
Kevin

Review Slip

Fishing With Foster
The Legend Begins…
by Turner Bowman
Illustrations by Larry Brooks
80 pages   9 1/4" x 12 1/4"
Four-color photos and illustrations throughout
Foster's Fishing Words (glossary)
ISBN: 0-9677118-0-0
$21.95 hardcover (laminate cover)
For ages 5 and up
Publication date: August 2000

For additional information, to request a b&w or color photograph, or to arrange an interview with Foster or Mr. Bowman, please contact: Kate Bandos, KSB Promotions • **800-304-3269** • KSBPromo@aol.com

Please send copies of any review or mention to Always Kids Publishing, P.O. Box 701790, San Antonio, TX 78270.

Fishing With Foster is available by calling toll-free, **800-603-6041** or visit www.fishingwithfoster.com.

fishing early i for me.
Alexandra

Every time i go fishing The fish are sleeping.
Delaney

Why do I have to be so quiet, fish don't even have any ears.
Kayla

I am going to be a fishing cheerleader.
Cara

I always catch bigger fish than my DAD
JACK

Mom Lets me go fishing so L. :p really
Logan

D1071164

FOSTER'S
Rules of the game

Have fun

Prayers do work

Never stop being a kid

Adults must bait our hooks

A kid must catch the biggest fish

Put on sunscreen, like a million proof

When the fish won't bite, talk to them

Everyone wears their lucky life jacket

Bring some good fish catching music

Never weigh your fish, always guess

All the bass you catch, let them go

Don't ever forget your fishing pole

A kid has to catch the most fish

Firetiger lures are the best

Dads will clean the fish

Put the drain plug in the boat

Grown-ups need a license to fish

No complaining if the fish are sleeping

Pack plenty of peanut butter and jelly's

Missing a little school to go fishing, it's OK

Always Kids Publishing

Special Thanks

To my Dad for showing me how much fun it is to fish.
To Mr. Jay for showing me how much more fun it is to Catch Fish!
To my Mom for being a great mom and letting me and Dad go fish.
To my sisters for being the best fishing buddies a kid can have.
To God for all his blessings.

Illustrations by Larry Brooks
Graphic design by Terri Christie
Pre-Press by Guru EFX
Photograph on page 71 by Jennifer Jennings

Printed in the United States of America

Library of Congress Card Number: 00-190807

ISBN 0-9677118-0-0

Published by Always Kids Publishing,
18160 Hwy. 281 North, Ste. 108, PNB 221
San Antonio, TX 78232

FISHING
WITH
FOSTER

FISH ON

 = Foster's Secret Fishing Tips

If there are any fishing words, you don t know. Check out my dictionary in the back of the book.

FISHING with FOSTER

Hi, I'm Foster. I'm a kid just like you and I live in this place called Texas. I have a great Mom and Dad and three awesome little sisters, Brennan, Cara and Bridgette. I really like going to school. I like going to Sunday school and learning about the Bible and going to my real school and learning about all kinds of great stuff like reading and writing and math and even science. I have a lot of fun playing with my friends on the playground too. Those monkey bars are a blast. I know the best thing you can do in school is to make good grades and don't get put in timeout.

You know I like other things too, like playing baseball and basketball and football and gymnastics and playing flashlight tag with my friends is really a blast. I even find a little time to watch the fishing shows and the Nascar races on TV. Mom says it is more than a little time, she says it's more like all the time.

But you know what I like most of all? I like to fish. No, I love to fish! I started fishing when I was two and I like it more now than ever. When I grow up I want to be a fisherman because fishermen never grow up, they get to be kids forever. This book is about fishing and it's for kids and dad's who still act like us kids.

Fishing with Foster started a long time ago, like when there were still dinosaurs running around. That's when my Grandaddy Bubba showed my Dad how much fun fishing was when he was a kid. Now my Dad is showing me and I'm telling you all about it. Fishing is the best fun a kid can have. I hope this book is the first of many fishing trips we'll be taking together.

Lets Go Fishing!!

Foster

Sometimes Casting Can Be Pretty Hairy

When I was real little I went to this Kidfish thing in Marble Falls. There was a fishing contest for kids, some arts and crafts for the mom's, some food for the dad's, a big carnival, lots of cotton candy and a casting contest. Guess you know I went to the fishing contest first. We used these slimy worms for bait and all anyone caught was some turtles and a couple of perch. All the big fish were sleeping. It was still fun though, watching that red and white cork, hoping the monsters would wake up for lunch. Oh well, no such luck.

So I decided to try out the casting contest. This old fisherman handed me a little kids fishing pole and told me to cast this lure with no hooks into the hula hoop. There was a pink one that was really close, another green one pretty far away and a bright orange one way, way far away. I started to cast at the orange one and the man started laughing and said "No, no son that target is for the grown ups, you can throw at the pink one." Well that pink one was just too close, so I just threw that lure as far as I could and it went really far, I mean it flew over the pink one and the green one and even the orange one.

A really long way away there was a bunch of people standing on this boat and my lure lands right in the middle of this lady's really big yellow hair. Man she started screaming cause she didn't know what had got a hold of her. The fisherman running the contest couldn't believe how far I threw that lure and when he saw where it landed, he said "Well this contest is over" and handed me the trophy. When I reeled that lure in Dad said it was too bad that lady wasn't wearing a wig or I would have won the trophy for the biggest catch too. I always catch something every time I go fishing. Maybe not always a fish, but always something.

Cast with the wind instead of against it, your lure will go really far.

The Fishless Pond

Me and my Dad and Uncle Tracy and Uncle Chuck and Mr. Larry went to this old ranch to do some mowing. There was this little pond where the cows drank water but the cows were gone now. Dad wanted to teach me how to fish so he gave me this little Snoopy-fishing pole. I mean I was only like 2 years old.

Dad said this pond was a good place to learn how to cast cause there were no trees for me to get hung up in. "Yeah right, there were trees everywhere." Then he told me there was no fish in the pond either. I asked him why we were fishing where there was no fish. He said it was good practice. I told him we should practice where there were some fish. Mr. Larry said I was right.

I was using a little lure called a fat rat. It didn't look like a rat, much less a fat rat. It was a tiny green and red lure with big hooks. Why did my lure have hooks if there were not any fish here anyway? I guess so I could catch some grass on like every single cast. Dad would help me throw my lure out and I would reel it in. Dad finally let me throw it out by myself. If I got lucky that fat rat would hit the water before it hooked some brush or my pants or Dad's hat or the chair. Dad was now even thinking that the hooks were probably not such a good idea.

Dad and Mr. Larry were talking on the hill when something started pulling my line. I started yelling "Dad I got one, Dad I got one." Dad and Mr. Larry started laughing saying "Look, Foster thinks he has a fish, maybe an old tire but not a fish." Then right out in the middle of that old muddy cow tank this big fish with long whiskers rolled on top of the water and I have never seen my Dad run so fast.

Me and my little Snoopy-fishing pole were fighting a really big fish. I finally pulled that fish up on the ground and it was a huge catfish. My Dad grabbed the line and held that big cat up for everybody to see and that catfish was so big it broke the line and swam back into that so-called fishless pond. You see, I always believe that I am going to catch a fish on every cast, even if someone tells me there's not any fish. And you know, sometimes I do.

Who's the Best Fisherkid

You know kids have been catching fish for a long, long time. I bet the first fish that was caught was caught by a kid. My Grandaddy Bubba was a really good fisherkid, and man he loved to run. When he was a kid he would wake up when it was still dark outside and run from house to house, delivering newspapers. Then he would run to his secret fishing pond and catch some really huge fish and then he would run really fast and get to school before his first class started.

Grandaddy Bubba was also a great fisherdad. He taught my Dad how to fish when he was just a kid like me. My Dad caught his first fish when he was only six years old. It was a little bass. Even though my Dad is kind of old now he still acts like a kid everytime he catches a fish. My Dad was a good fisherkid that turned into a great fisherdad.

He started taking me fishing as soon as I could walk. I caught my first fish when I was really little. My first fish wasn't a perch or a little bass. It was a huge 5 pound striper that I caught while I was still wearing my pj's. Now who do you think is the best fisherkid in our family?

Not much has changed over the past few years. Dad and I still catch a lot of fish and mine are usually bigger. Now Dad has some even bigger problems. My little sisters Brennan and Cara are starting to catch bigger ones than him and it won't be long before my baby sister Bridgette is catching the big ones too. Dad says it's OK to catch bigger fish than him, as long as it doesn't happen all the time. He always reminds us that we have a pretty good teacher..... and you know what? He's right.

"You gotta be smiling when you can catch a striper this big wearing your pj's."

"Even a bad hair day can't stop Brennan from catching the big ones."

"My Dad was so proud of his first fish, a tiny, tiny, bass."

Four Cast and Four Monsters, I'm Good Luck

One day when I was only 2 years old my Dad, Uncle Bobby and our friend Jimmy went fishing at Braunig Lake. Uncle Bobby and Jimmy are the best fishing buddies a kid could have. They are like Batman and Robin. They are always showing me how to be a better fisherboy.

Well it wasn't long before Uncle Bobby hooked this bass that pulled really hard. When he finally got that fish in the boat it was Uncle Bobby's biggest bass ever, a 6 pounder. Man he was really pumped. Jimmy was so excited that he cast his lure so far that it went all the way over this huge tree and ended up hanging like 3 inches above the water. Then this huge bass came flying out of the water and ate his lure. That big bass scared Jimmy so much that he almost dropped his pole in the lake.

After a good battle he landed that bass and it was over 7 pounds. Jimmy said it was his biggest bass ever. Like we didn't know that already. On Jimmy's very next cast he caught another monster bass. When Dad saw how big that bass was he just dropped his pole and helped Jimmy get that big boy in the boat. Jimmy's bass was bigger than 8 pounds. Jimmy had now really caught his biggest bass ever. He was so excited he started doing the Jimmy Houston shuffle on the front of the boat.

While Jimmy was dancing my Dad told him he was going to catch an even bigger bass and Jimmy said, "Yeah right". Well Dad picked up his pole and started reeling in his orange crank bait and man, he had a fish on his line. Then that water exploded and it was the biggest bass you ever saw. They finally got that big baby in the boat and it weighed over 9 pounds. Dad tried to get me to hold it but I said "No Way Jose", cause it was just way too big.

The other fisherman around us could not believe the fish we just caught, I mean they could not catch even one. They really couldn't believe it when we let all those trophies go. After that day Dad and his friends told me that I was good luck and that they wanted me to go fishing with them every time they went. If there is one thing I have learned while being a kid, it is to always obey my Mom and Dad, especially when they tell me I have to go fishing.

When fishing in clear water use smaller lures and lighter fishing line.

"Me and my sisters are one heck of a crappie catching team."

"Before I go fishing I always do some work. My favorite work is mowing. Here I mowed the grass at my house and then I mowed the grass at the ranch and then I went fishing. It was a perfect day."

"Here I am with my biggest crappie ever and the next day Brennan caught a bigger one."

Top Dogs and Mr. Jay

One day me and my Dad went to the coast and fished with a man called Mr. Jay. His real name is Jay Watkins. Jay lives in a place called Rockport, Texas. Mr. Jay is the second best fisherman there is. Not as good as Jesus but better than everybody else. We went fishing in the bay at a place close to shore called the flats. I think they call it the flats because the water is real flat, not like the huge waves in the big ocean. The water in the flats is so clear that you can see all kinds of kool shells on the bottom. Then the wind blows and that clear green water turns to chocolate milk.

This day the wind didn't blow very much so we fished with Top Dogs. They're not real dogs, they're topwater lures that float and they don't really look like dogs at all. Mr. Jay likes to fish with lures. He always says "Foster if you learn to catch fish with lures you will never run out of bait." Top Dogs are so kool cause you can throw them a long way, like a million miles. You just reel em in and twitch your rod. The Top Dog does the rest. You better be ready cause when a monster red or trout eats that Top Dog you're gonna be shaking all over. Sometimes that dog is only like ten feet away when that big red explodes on it and you better hold onto your rod or that red will pull it right in the water. Jay is always telling me to hold on tight cause I'm holding his $400 rig. So what's the big deal?

A big red is really strong. I mean if they don't want to come in, there's nothing you can do. They will swim to the boat and then they make a run and swim away, leaving a mud trail like 5 feet wide. My arms were so tired after fighting one big red, how tired do you think I was after bringing in 10 of those big boys?

Fish like to eat Top Dogs the best when it is cloudy. Today it was cloudy all day, so we fished with the dogs until we were just too tired to catch anymore. This day we caught over 20 big reds and 25 nice trout, all on Top Dogs. Me and Mr. Jay, we make a pretty good fishing team.

Trout feed up and redfish feed down.

"This nice trout
came up
and smelled
the roses."

"Here is me and
Mr. Jay
with my first
Big Red
on a Top Dog."

"This big trout
hammered my
Top Dog. Mr. Kirk,
wearing his
big straw
hat, only
dreams about
catching
a trout as big
as mine."

Samson the Great Warrior

One of my most favorite places to fish is at the marina where we keep our boat. All kinds of fish live there, like perch, crappie, bass, carp, catfish and even some huge alligator gars. But the fish I always try to catch at the marina is Samson, the monster bass.

This is where I learned how to feel a fish bite my hook. Sometimes I fish with these little jigs with glitter in them. A jig is a little rubber thing that goes over your hook and looks like a baby octopus. When you feel the fish go tap, tap on your line, you pull up on your pole and you have a fish. A perch will tap just like a big bass.

The Big Preacherman at my church is Pastor Hagee and me and him, we fish just alike. We always think we are going to catch the next world record fish on every cast. I mean he always says, "If you're going to go fishing for Moby Dick, take the tarter sauce." To be a good fisherkid you have to think BIG.

This one day I was dropping my hot pink lucky lure in the different boat slips and I hooked a tree. I always get hung up fishing at the marina. Getting hung up is just part of being a kid. Dad can get my hooks unhung really good. He tells me practice makes perfect. Dad came over and reached down in the cold, dark water to unhook my line and all of the sudden this huge bass jumps like 2 feet from his head. I think my Dad had a little heart attack. You see I wasn't hung up on an old rotten tree, I was hung up on Sampson, the huge marina bass that I had been trying to catch for more than 2 years.

Well Samson jumped at least 5 times, shaking and baking, trying to throw my lure out of his mouth. There must have been 10 people watching me battling Samson. Finally, that big boy got tired and my Dad grabbed him by the lip and lifted him out of the water. Samson was finally mine. Those people had never seen a bass that big. They wanted me to take him home for dinner. No way. Samson is a great warrior, I let him go knowing that we would do battle again soon, very soon.

Check the end of your line after you catch a fish or a tree.

Little T and Her Lucky Fishing Glove

I ran into my friend Little T at the lake and told her I was going fishing at the marina later in the day. She said she wanted to go. Little T is so kool, she wanted to fish with me. I don't know too many girls that like to fish like Little T does. I know my sisters love to fish but hey, they're my sisters, they were born to fish. I think girls that like to fish are awesome.

When I got to the marina Little T was already there and oh boy, she was wearing her lucky fishing glove. She only wears that glove when she is serious about catching some fish. I guess she knew if we were fishing together those fish didn't stand a chance. I walked up to Little T and saw that she was fishing for perch. You won't believe what she was using for bait. She was using ham. The same stuff you put on a sandwich. I thought you gotta be kidding, until she showed me how many perch she had caught, like more than fifty. Those perch must really like that ham. Now I knew why she was wearing her fishing glove.

Well I was using my little jigs, like I always do and I hooked a really big one. I was yelling and screaming and Little T came over to see what I had. She thought I only had a little perch. Then that big mouth bass jumped like ten feet out of the water and Little T about fell in the lake. I didn't know how we were going to land that big fish. There was no way I was going to grab it and Brennan and her dip net were nowhere to be found. Then Little T said, "I'll grab him with my fishing glove." She reached down and grabbed that bass and pulled it out of the water. We couldn't believe how big that bass was.

Man I am glad she had her lucky fishing glove on. We let that bass go so he could get even bigger and we could catch him again on another day. Little T then looked over at me and said "Foster, I'll trade you some of my ham for one of your jigs." Little T is a pretty smart fishergirl.

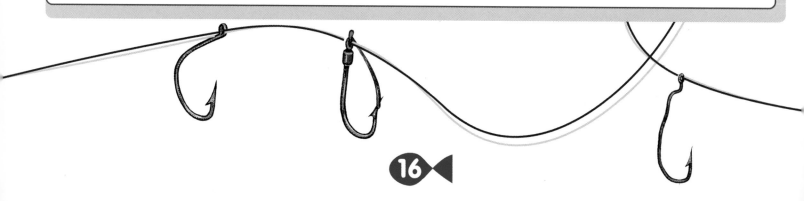

"A bass that big really makes you smile."

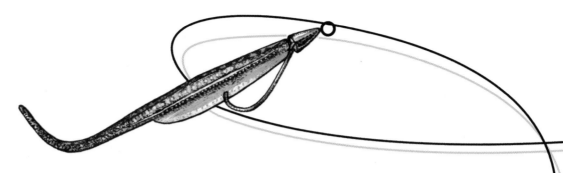

I got a Fish, not the Anchor Rope

One summer day we were fishing at the coast using live shrimp and bass assassin lures for bait. We had our most fun trying to grab those live shrimp in the bucket, I mean those shrimp can jump like a wild bull frog. Once again, the wind was blowing about a hundred miles an hour. That wind made my line go on the other side of the boat and under the anchor rope.

As I was reeling in my lure a fish came up and ate it. I told Dad I had a big fish and he said, "You don't have a fish you have the anchor." Once again I knew different. Dad pulled in the anchor rope and my line was wrapped around it, just like he said. But I also had a big fish on my line too. We were both right. Somehow Dad unhooked my line from the anchor rope without breaking it. Then that fish made a run and I didn't think he was ever going to stop. No matter how hard I would pull, that fish was not coming in. Was it a big bull red or a 30 inch monster trout?

Finally, after like forever, my leader was at the boat. That fish was making the water so muddy we couldn't see what it was. Dad grabbed the leader and started to pull it in when all of the sudden this huge, dark, gray stingray came flying out of the water. His poisonous tail must have been 5 feet long. I don't know who was more scared, us or him. Dad didn't even try to unhook the stingray, he just cut the line and let him go. The first fish I ever caught in the ocean was a big scary stingray. A little while later I caught my second fish in the ocean, a nice 22 inch redfish. Guess how many fish everyone else caught this day? Two less than me. When it comes to fishing, I'm pretty lucky.

When fishing in the bays the best fishing is when the tide is moving, either in or out.

"Here I am showing my friend Eric how to practice fishing in the yard."

"Another big bass I caught with Brennan by my side."

"Here is my cousin Layne with a real kool looking fish. They call this fish a sheepshead. But you know, I have never seen a striped sheep before. It looks like a zebrafish to me."

"Just because I love to catch big fish doesn't mean I have to like holding them, especially when the fish is almost as big as I am."

"Me and Taylor are fishing on the pier in the ocean. We're not catching much but we sure are looking good."

"This is what kidluck is all about."

Waders and the Stingray Shuffle

Me and my friend Gunner and our Dad's went wade fishing at the beach. Wade fishing is when you walk in the water and fish. I told Dad we should be fishing in our boat. He said our boat was broke. It seems like every time we have a fishing trip planned our boat is broke and in the shop. Even when we get our boat out of the shop we have to put it right back in. Dad should probably get rid of his boat storage and just leave his boat at the shop, I mean that is where it stays most of the time anyway.

So if you don't have a boat you will probably do some wade fishing and if you do have a boat you will definitely be doing some wade fishing. I know our boat would probably never go to the shop if Dad could find a way not to run over every single stump, sandbar, oyster reef and huge rock that is in the water.

Today was my first time to go wading. It was freezing cold and the wind was blowing, like always. Why does the wind always blow at the beach anyway? When the water is cold you need to wear waders. Waders are plastic pants you wear over your clothes so you won't get wet and cold. Unless you fall down and your waders fill up with water. Then you're gonna freeze. One thing for sure is that if that happens you can't ever go home and tell your mom, she probably will never let you and your dad go fishing again. Always wear your lifejacket when you go wading and make sure your dad or somebody bigger is with you all the time.

When you are wading in the ocean you should always do the stingray shuffle. When you are walking, be sure to shuffle your feet and don't pick them up and down. You see if you step on a stingray they can sting you but when you shuffle your feet you will kick them and they will swim away.

Wade fishing is kool because you are walking around fishing in the water with the fish. Sometimes to catch a fish you have to be a fish. This day we had a blast. We caught some hard head catfish, a few crabs, a tire, an old air conditioner and a pretty good cold. Dad always tells me that it's great to fish in the ocean cause you never know what you are going to catch. Man was he ever right.

When fishing in muddy water use big, noisy lures with bright colors.

"Wading with the 12th Man from Texas A&M!"

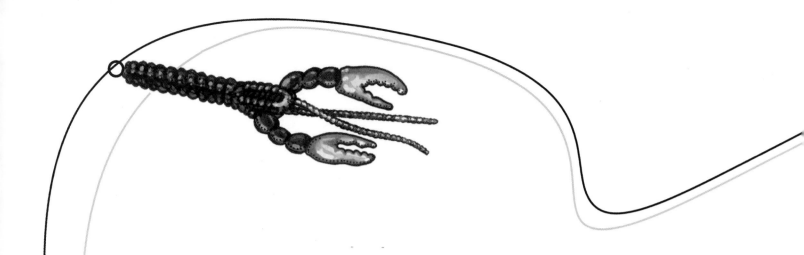

Brennan and the Monster Rainbow

Every year we go to this thing called The Boat Show. There is lots of kool stuff to do at the boat show but what we like to do the most is fish for trout. A long time ago Grandaddy Bubba used to take my Dad fishing at the same trout tank we fish at. They have thousands of rainbows in that fishing tank and they always have one monster rainbow. They blow a horn and you start fishing. You fish with these flies that are not real flies, they kind of look like bugs with hooks.

My sister, Brennan, put her fly right in front of the big monster rainbow's mouth and she was talking to it saying "Here fishy, fishy, here pretty fishy" and all the sudden that huge rainbow opened its mouth and ate her fly. It started pulling so hard Dad had to grab Brennan before she got pulled into the water. Brennan was hanging on real good. I think it was because she was too scared to let go. All of the sudden that huge rainbow fish came flying out of the water and when it landed everyone got soaked.

Well that was it for Brennan, she dropped her pole and took off running and never looked back until she had a hold of Mom's leg. I couldn't believe Brennan had lost her rainbow. I turned around to see where that fish was and you won't believe it. It was in the big fisherman's net. He got it in the net right when she dropped her pole. Brennan had her monster rainbow! She wouldn't get near that fish though, it was just too big. That fisherman asked her if she wanted to take it home and she looked at him with big tears in her eyes and said "Why don't you just put him back so another kid can catch him, maybe a bigger kid." That's my Brennan.

When your dad lets you throw the anchor overboard make sure there is a rope tied to it before you throw it in.

Follow that Cork

While we were at the beach, me and my friend Huntleigh and our Dad's went fishing for speckled trout and redfish with Mr. Jay. This day the trout were not very hungry. The water was really hot and that makes the trout real sleepy. The good news is that the redfish like to eat all the time, even in hot water. All you have to do is find them.

So we started looking for them. Mr. Jay has eyes like Superman, I mean he can see those fish really far away, even underwater. We were riding in the boat and Mr. Jay spotted a bright pink cork in the water. He stopped the boat and told us to throw our lures over by that cork. We did and when those lures hit the water, a bunch of huge reds jumped all over them. Everybody hooked a big red at the same time. It didn't matter what lures we threw, gold spoon, top dog, assassin, whatever, the reds were eating our lures like me and Huntleigh munching on some chicken nuggets at McDonalds.

Those big reds were making us run all over that boat. Jay said he wasn't sure if we had the reds or if the reds had us. We finally got all 5 reds in the boat. It was awesome! After a bunch of high fives we realized we had a big problem, the cork was gone. We had to find that cork. We drove around slowly, looking and looking until one of us spotted that cork. It was as much fun finding the cork as it was catching those big reds.

You see there were thousands of golden redfish in that school and one of them was hooked to that cork. When that school of reds would be swimming, the cork would go under the water and when they would stop swimming, the cork would pop up. Then we would just drift towards the cork and when we got close enough we would cast and hang on tight cause we were going to catch a big red. We finally went home cause we were totally tired from catching so many huge reds. Some days you out smart the fish, most days the fish out smart you. Today it was our day to win.

When fishing with a topwater lure don't set the hook when you see the fish splash, wait until you feel the fish pull on your line, then give it a Power Team Pull!

"That Big 4 spot Red ate the whole Top Dog."

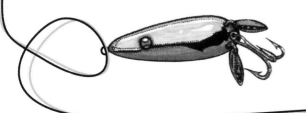

Little Jack has Kidluck

I have a friend named Little Jack. One day I went fishing with him and his dad. They have the same name so we call them Little Jack and Big Jack. This day was a good day because Little Jack caught his very first fish, a nice 2 pound bass. Man was he happy, but I think his dad was even more happy. Little Jack caught five more nice bass this day and his dad couldn't catch any. Finally after about 3 hours of fishing Big Jack finally hooked a fish. That fish didn't put up much of a fight and when he finally got it in...man it was a whopper. All of 3 inches long. It was the littlest bass you ever saw. I mean his lure was bigger than the fish.

How can Big Jack, this really strong guy like Hercules, catch one tiny, tiny bass and his 3 year old son, Little Jack catch 5 nice bass. Well it's this thing called Kidluck and all kids have it. You see, a lot of good things always happen to kids and that is what Kidluck is about.

Me and my friends always catch more and bigger fish than our Dad's. I think they always take us fishing so they can tell their friends that they caught some really nice fish. When really it was the kids who caught the fish. One of the best things about fishing is listening to our Dad's tell their buddies how many fish they caught. Sometimes my Dad's stories sound like he caught every fish in the lake. Oh well, as long as they keep taking us fishing they can tell their friends any stories they want. You see we will always have one thing on our side, Kidluck, and that's the best thing a kid can have.

The best fishing days are when there is a full moon and when there is no moon.

"Catching perch is a blast. You can catch like a hundred at a time."

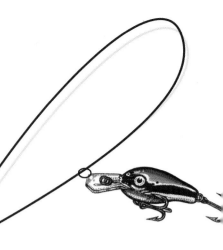

"Me and Logan with a couple of Kingfish we caught in the big ocean. Those fish are as big as us."

"This is so Brennan, a nice white bass in one hand and some candy in the other."

"Here I am with my first fishing pole. Dad got me the pole and the baseball. Mom got me the Speedo."

"This is how you hold a bass so they won't get away."

My Favorite Fishing Knots & Fishing Reels

Knots are really important because the only thing between you and your trophy fish is the knot that ties your line to your lure.

It's pretty smart to always let your dad or a grown up tie your knot so that if it ever does comes loose you can blame it on them.

This is a Topwater Knot

This knot is the best for topwater lures. It gives the lure a lot of action.

This is a Underwater Knot

Use this knot for tying all your swimming lures and hooks to your line.

This is a Leader Knot

Use this knot when you are tying two fishing lines together.

Spincaster Reel

These reels are really good for kids and for mom's and dad's that are learning to fish. Almost all of my fish I have caught using this reel. These reels come in all kinds of kool colors and they are pretty easy to use, with a little practice of course.

Spinning Reel

You fish with these after you know how to fish with a Spincaster. Spinning reels are great for kids and grown ups. The best thing about Spinning reels is that you can fish all day, catch lots of fish and never get a birdsnest.

Baitcasting Reel

These are what the really good fisherman use. It takes a lot of practice to cast a baitcaster and not get a birdsnest, like on every cast. My Dad always blames his birdsnest on the wind or the lure or the sun, always something. I think he just needs to practice more and take me with him.

Foster's Lucky "13"

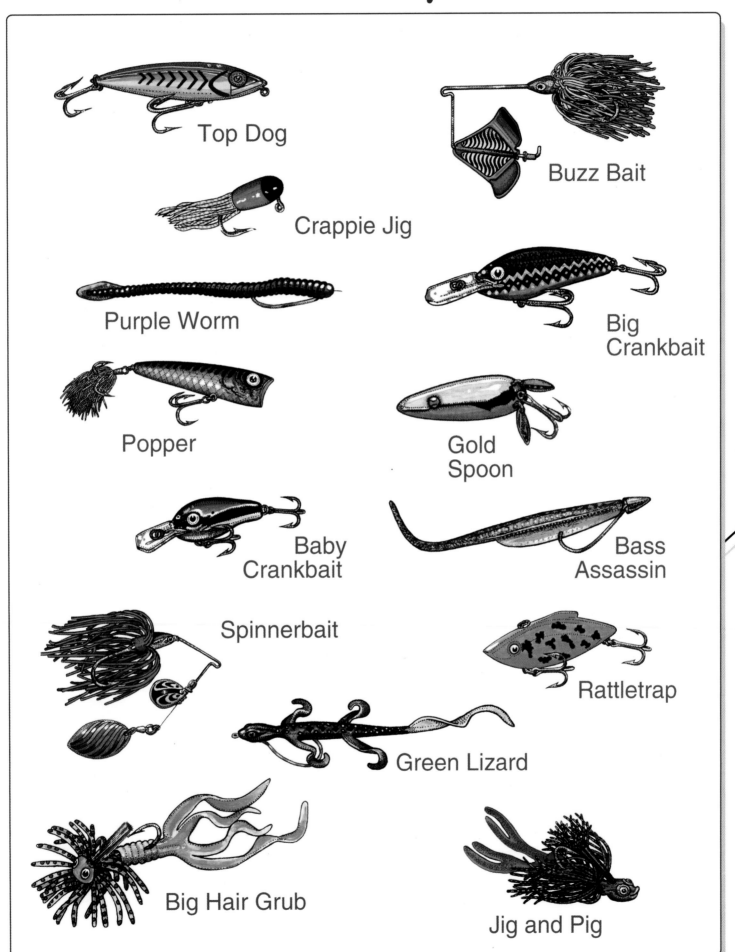

Top Dog

Buzz Bait

Crappie Jig

Purple Worm

Big Crankbait

Popper

Gold Spoon

Baby Crankbait

Bass Assassin

Spinnerbait

Rattletrap

Green Lizard

Big Hair Grub

Jig and Pig

Worm Fishing and the Power Team Pull

When it gets hot the fish like to go in deeper water cause it is cooler down there. That is when it is time to fish with a worm. There are two kinds of worm fishing, a Texas Rig, named after my Dad cause he lives in Texas and a Carolina Rig, named after my Uncle Tracy cause he lives in Carolina. I guess if I ever move to Alabama then there will be a third kind of worm fishing, the Alabama Rig.

These worms we fish with are not like the kind you find in the street when it rains and they are not like the slimy ones crawling around in that yucky dirt at the store. These are plastic worms, but they feel more like rubber to me. Worms come in all kinds of colors: Blue, red, black, green, yellow, purple and some even have glitter in them. They have funny names too like Tukeela Sunrise, Firetiger, Pumpkinseed, Junebug, Watermelon and they even have a worm called a French Fry. You know the bass love to eat that one. They also make worms that look like lizards and crawdads. You know how to pick what worm to use? You do what Uncle Frankie always does, you asked the guy at the grocery store what they're biting on.

Fishing with a worm is pretty easy, you slowly move your pole up and down and when you feel a fish go tap, tap you lower your rod, count to two and give it a Power Team Pull. I named my hook set after the Power Team because they are the strongest guys in the World. They go to schools and churches and tell everyone how great Jesus is and then they rip telephone books in half, break baseball bats and roll up frying pans like a tortilla with their hands. When you hook a fish with a Power Team Pull they are probably never going to get away.

Sometimes worm fishing can be kind of boring if the fish are sleeping. I think worm fishing is better for older people that can fish all day long and never even have a bite and still act like they are having fun. With kids, if we're not having fun, we just tell you. I mean if I make five cast with a worm and no bites, I'm putting on a firetiger-topwater or crank bait and I'm gonna wake those babies up. Dad likes it when I do that cause he says I scare all the fish to him. All I'm really doing is giving him have a chance to catch as many as me.

Spinning reels are great for throwing little lures a long way.

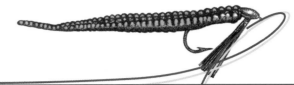

My Minnow Girls

How many guys are lucky enough to have two little sisters who love to fish. How many guys are even luckier to have one sister who loves to catch the minnows and another who loves to put the minnow on your hook.

One day we were catching crappie at the marina. We were not fishing for crappie, we were catching crappie. There is a big difference in fishing and catching. Catching is much better. We were using live minnows for bait. Dad was putting those minnows on our hooks as fast as he could but he couldn't keep up cause we were catching so many fish. Dad told me that I had to learn how to put those minnows on my own hook cause we were wearing him out. I tried it and the hardest thing was catching those quick little suckers in that bucket. It's not easy holding onto those slippery dudes either. I mean those minnows were always slipping out of my hands and then I would have to catch them while they were flipping and flopping on the dock.

Well, I'm reeling in this crappie and I hear my sister Brennan say "Look Foster I did it." She had caught a minnow and put it on her hook all by herself. She thought she was so kool, and she really was. Every time I needed a minnow she would put her rod down and grab a minnow and put it on my hook. Then she would grab her pole and she would always have a big crappie on her line. Brennan always catches really big fish. Then my other sister Cara, who is only 3, started catching the minnows and giving them to Brennan and she would put them on my hook. My sisters were a great team and they were having a blast too. The greatest thing Brennan said to me was, "Foster, we're your minnow girls." Boy do I love my sisters.

When a fish attacks your lure it will attack the front of the lure.

Life Jackets Bring Good Luck

A lot of kids have things that bring them good luck. I have my lucky life jackets. One day my Dad took me wadefishing at the beach. A cold front blew in and man it was freezing. It was so cold I had to wear like three pairs of pants, four shirts and my waders. I made a couple of cast and then I hooked a really nice fish. I was fighting that fish when a big boat drove by and made waves that were like 10 feet tall. Those waves knocked me down and my waders got full of water and I was really scared. Then I realized that I was floating because I had on my lucky life jacket.

Dad ran over and picked me up and helped me to shore. We dumped all the water out of my waders and man I was cold as a snowman. I couldn't believe it. I had lost my favorite fishing pole and the big fish that was on my line. I started running toward the car where it was warm, cause I was freezing. Then I saw something that the wave washed up on the beach. I ran over to check it out and it was my fishing pole. I picked it up and I still had that fish on my line, can you believe that? A couple of minutes later I landed a really nice trout. It was a really good thing that I was wearing my life jacket.

You see, I can swim really good but I don't go fishing without wearing my life jacket. It is just like I don't get in a car without wearing my seatbelt. You know every fish I have ever caught I was wearing one of my lucky life jackets. My sisters and all my friends and all the kids who go fishing with me wear their lucky life jackets all the time. Whenever you go fishing or swimming you need to wear a life jacket.

You know how many fish me and my friends have caught without wearing a life jacket? NONE. You know how many fish me and my friends have caught while wearing our lucky life jackets? TONS. When you wear your life jacket you will catch a lot of fish and if you hook a world record fish that pulls you in the water, no problem, because you will have your lucky life jacket on. Be a kool fisherkid, always wear a life jacket.

"It takes as much luck to catch the little ones, as it does to catch the big ones."

"My friend Jared and his 'Field of Dreams' Nothing but blue sky, green grass and a stringer full of 3 pound bass."

"Huntleigh always wanted to catch a big Trout, and with his life jacket on, he did."

39

What the Heck is a Gasper Goo?

I was fishing at the marina and I hooked a really big fish. This older man working on his boat saw my rod bending and came over to see what I had. I told him that I had a pretty good one. He said "Sorry son, you wish you had a fish that big, all you really have is a tree or the dock." I do not know why nobody ever believes me when I tell them I have a fish.

I told that man I had a really big one and he just laughed at me. He reached down and grabbed my line to try and unhook it and about that time that fish that wasn't supposed to be there made a run and about pulled that man in the water. I was hanging on to that pole and yelling for somebody to help me. Finally, Mr. Michael came over and helped me get that monster fish out of the water. Mr. Michael knows that when I say I have a fish, I have a fish.

When I saw that fish I couldn't believe how ugly it was. I mean that fish was huge and man it was really ugly. I had never seen anything that looked like that before. They told me I had just caught a Gasper Goo. I mean what the heck is a Gasper Goo? I guess that fish got such a funny name cause when you see one...you gotta laugh.

That man that almost got pulled in the water said, "You know son, I'm sorry, I really thought you were hung up." I just wonder when these people are ever going to start believing me. I mean I am Foster the fisherboy.

When the sun comes out the fish swim to deeper water.

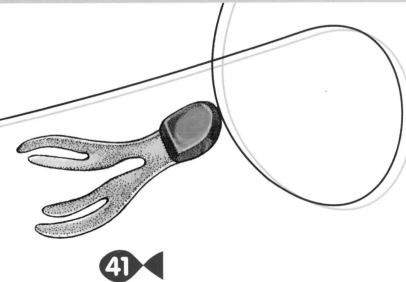

"Me and Brennan catching some stripers. Brennan is probably the first girl to ever catch a fish with a pink bow in her hair."

"Here is little Jack with his first fish, a real nice bass."

"Here is Brennan teaching her friend Brandon how to fish. Look at that big crappie. I don't think Brennan knows how to catch a little fish."

"Here are my friends, Darby and Preston. This is Darby's first bass and man it's a nice one. Preston, he loves those grape sodas, even more than fishing. I mean he had a purple mustache all day long."

"This old man at the store told me that if I wanted to catch a fish I had to be a fish, today we were going fishing for some mud cats."

Started a Little Early...
Stopped a Little Late

We went to this Boat Show in Austin so Mom and Dad could check out the new boats and me and my little sisters could check out the cotton candy machines and the fishing tank. At this boat show they had a huge glass swimming pool full of big catfish with long whiskers. I knew I could catch those catfish. I mean I could see them swimming around in the pool. If I can catch fish in a lake and in the ocean without ever seeing them, catching these babies was going to be a piece of cake.

I gave the lady my ticket and went in and grabbed a pole. They told us not to start fishing until the whistle blew. Well I was standing there smelling that popcorn, waiting for that whistle to blow when my bait fell in the water and man I had a fish on my line. How did that happen? All the kids were coming in and waiting to start fishing and I'm fighting this big old cat. The lady tells everyone over the speaker to not start fishing until the whistle blows, then she says "Oh look, that little boy already has one, how did that happen?"

I mean they unhooked that fish for me and I caught another one and another one and another one and then she told everyone to stop fishing and before I could get my hook out of the water, I hooked another one. Everyone left the fishing area and I'm still fighting that last big cat. They said they had never seen anyone catch two catfish in one five minute fishing period, much less five.

You see, Dad always tells me that whenever I do something I need to start a little early and stop a little late. I think he was probably talking about mowing the grass or washing the car or painting the fence, you know, workerman stuff. Well today I did a little catfishing and just like Dad always told me to do, I started a little early and I stopped a little late.

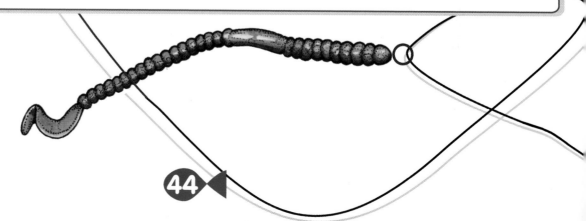

Always put on lots of sunscreen when you go fishing.

The Magnificent Seven

One summer we went to the beach for a vacation. Dad always brings his boat. I think the main reason we take the boat is to carry all our beach stuff like toys and chairs and tents and food and drinks and lots of other stuff. One day Dad and Uncle Chuck said they wanted to go fishing in the bay. Mom told Dad the only way he could go fishing was if he took all seven of us kids with him. He was really pretty lucky that Brennan and Cara were too little or it could have been nine kids.

Well we got some live shrimp and some croakers for bait and headed out. Five minutes later we found the flats. Once again we were stuck in six inches of water thanks to my Dad's driving. Dad told us he had found the hot spot. Yeah right. They put bait on all seven of our poles and cast them out for us. There were corks bobbing up and down everywhere. Uncle Chuck and Dad were going crazy trying to keep a live shrimp on everybody's hook. The fish were stealing the shrimp faster than they could put them on.

All the kids made a pact that we were not going to the beach until every kid had caught a fish. It was going to be a pretty long day. We had been fishing for like 3 hours and we had caught no fish. Finally Kayla caught one, then Acacia caught one, then Charlotte caught one and Kadie caught one, too. Every girl had caught a fish and the boys had none. Something was not right here. Finally Logan caught a trout and a little while later Layne hooked a little red. Now I was the only one without a fish. It was really hot out there and everyone wanted to go to the beach. I had to catch a fish and soon.

All the kids were talking to me saying, "Come on Foster. you can do it, you can catch one." Then I started talking to the fish like I always do and sure enough, a Big Red heard me. The line started screaming off my reel. The kids wanted to help me fight that fish but I told them that I could do it by myself. After like thirty minutes I finally got that big red in the boat and The Magnificent Seven......was headed for the beach.

Go Acacia

Go Charlotte

Go Kadie

Where's Foster?

Go Kayla

Go Layne

Go Logan

Trolling the Trees for a Big Old Red

Dad likes to take me and my sisters fishing at his secret lake. This lake is great because it has stripers, big bass, catfish and redfish, like you catch in the ocean. Dad always takes us fishing when it is still dark outside. He says that we need to be fishing when the fish wake up cause that is when they are really hungry. My sisters and I keep telling Dad we should wait and fish for the late sleepers. He acts like he doesn't hear us.

For three years we have tried to catch a big redfish at this lake and we have had no luck at all. Today we were trolling with downriggers using gold colored spoons for lures. The redfish live in the trees in real deep water. Well, our spoons went real deep into the trees and we caught plenty, plenty of trees. After catching four or five trees my Dad turns the same color as a big red. Since we were only catching trees this day, like everyday, we took a little nap. Dad always brings us pillows and blankets for napping and peanut butter and jelly's for snacking.

Dad woke us up because he needed some help, he had hooked another treefish. I grabbed the pole and he kept backing up the boat to the tree and the tree kept moving farther and farther away. I said "Dad this is not a tree, it's a monster red." At first he just laughed, then he realized I was right, as usual. Me and my sisters were now fighting our biggest fish ever. I looked up and saw Brennan talking on Dad's cell phone. She was telling Mom about our monster red. Dad said that for sure Grandaddy Bubba just rolled over in his grave. Our big red was getting close to the boat and Dad asked me if I knew where the dip net was. I told him it was in our backyard where me and Caleb were catching butterflies the other day. He was not a happy camper.

All the other boats were watching us as we tried to get that big red in the boat. Finally that big dude started getting tired and we all pulled up on that pole and Dad reached in the water and grabbed that big red with his hands and threw him in the boat. He was so huge. All the people in the other boats started clapping and cheering. I gave my sisters a big hug and we all gave Dad a big bear hug and lots of high fives. Man, all those trips and all those trees and finally we had a monster red.

Use a trailer hook when fishing with a spinnerbait or buzzbait. Two hooks are better than one.

"Wow!! Look at the size of that Black Drum fish. Man Gunner, you are the King Fisherkid."

"How much Kidluck does my buddy Josh have? Looks like about 8 pounds 7 ounces to me. Now that is a LARGEMOUTH BASS!!"

"Caleb's Grandpa took him fishing and the final score was Caleb 3 bass, Grandpa zero. Some things never change!"

"Just another great day for me and Mr. Jay."

"My friends Jaimie and Andrew came all the way from this place across the ocean called Scotland to fish with me. They thought the fishing in Texas was awesome but the hundred degree heat was way too hot."

"Taylor is really smiling after he caught his first big trout."

Bass Pros should Listen to Kids

My sisters Brennan and Cara and my cousins Layne and Logan and me went fishing on Travis Lake. It was an awesome spring day. It was cool, the wind wasn't blowing and the fish were going to bite, I just knew it.

This day we caught and released 35 bass in less than 3 hours. Some of the bass were little and some were over 3 pounds. We were trolling with four rods out all the time. We caught all of our fish on little firetiger crank baits. Sometimes we caught two at a time, that's called a double. Sometimes we caught three at a time, that's called a triple. Once we caught four bass at one time, that's called kidluck.

There was a bass contest going on and all these guys with patches on their shirts and real kool, fast and shiny boats were fishing all around us. You see they were doing a whole lot of fishing and we were doing a whole lot of catching. After watching us kids catch so many bass they finally came over and asked us how in the world we were catching so many fish.

It was hard to hear them because our fish catching music was playing so loud. Our favorite fishing music is Trout Fishing in America. We always catch lots of fish when we sing and dance to "When I was a Dinosaur" and "Pico de Gallo". When we need to catch a really big fish we put on "We are the Dinosaurs".

We showed the fishermen our little crank baits and then we each pulled a big bass out of the livewell and they just stood there with their mouths wide open, they couldn't believe it. They could have easily won the contest with our fish. We decided to help those fishermen out, so we let all our fish go right in front of them and told them we hoped they would catch them and win first place.

The next day we went back to our favorite spot and guess who was there and guess what lures they were using? Do you think if those fisherguys won the contest they would tell everyone that they got their tips from a bunch of kids? Not a chance.

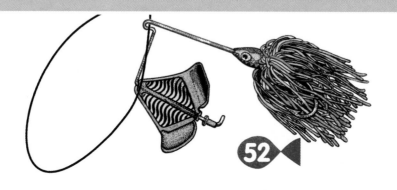

Fish with topwaters early in the morning, right before dark and when it is cloudy. Start around Easter and don't stop until Thanksgiving.

Freddy and Nothing but a Bunch a Bones

Me and my Dad decided we were going to set out a trotline at the lake. A trotline is a long string that has a bunch of hooks tied to it. You tie each end of that string to a rope that has a rock on the bottom and a rainbow colored plastic milk jug on the top, so you won't ever lose it. I have no idea why they call it a trotline. Anyway, you put perch or stinky bait on the hooks and leave them out overnight. I mean how easy can fishing be. You set out your trotline and put your bait on, go home and play with your friends and then come back in a few hours and see if you caught any fish.

This day Dad and I set the trotline in our favorite cove. This isn't our favorite cove because of the fish we have caught, it is our favorite cove because of this 15 pound bass named Freddie that we have lost. I have hooked Freddie three times and every time he has broke my line. I thought maybe Freddie had some big catfish friends that live here too.

We took our flashlights and went out late at night and put bait on the trotline. The next day we went to check it out and see what we caught and you won't believe what we found. Nothing, our trotline was gone. I mean it was there yesterday and gone today. Our trotline was gone and all the monster catfish on it were gone too. I told Dad that Freddie probably took the whole trotline with him.

Well we never did any more trotlining for the rest of the year. The next year we went fishing for Freddie at our favorite cove and I hooked a nice bass on a silver and black popper. As I was reeling him in you won't believe what I saw. Two feet under the water was our rainbow milk jug. I told dad what I saw and he just said, "You gotta be kidding." You see our trotline had not gone anywhere, all that had happened was that the lake had come up a couple of feet. I decided to check the trotline and when I pulled it up you won't believe what we caught. Nothing but a bunch of bones.

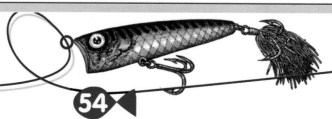

After casting a topwater let the wave ring get to 6 feet wide before twitching your rod.

Catfish after Church

I always wanted to catch a catfish at the lake. Me and Dad and my sisters must have tried catfishing 5 or 6 times and we never caught any. We watch the catfishing guys on TV and do just what they say and we still don't catch any. Those catfish are way too smart. When we fish for catfish we put this really bad smelling goop on our hook, put a weight on our line and throw it out there and wait and wait and wait and wait and then we reel in our line and our bait is gone.

One Sunday after church was over I went crappie fishing at the marina and I put four poles out. Two for me and two for my sisters. All of the sudden one of my poles was headed into the lake, then another and another. I had a fish on every pole. Finally Brennan and Cara came running up and grabbed two of the poles and I had the other two. I reeled in one of my poles and it had a nice crappie on it. Then I started reeling in the other pole and that fish started taking line and it wouldn't stop.

After about twenty minutes that fish finally got tired but not until he had really wore me out. I thought it had to be a big old carp. When that fish finally made it to the surface I couldn't believe it, it was a monster yellow cat. I told Cara to grab it and she said "Yeah right, you grab it Foster the Fisherboy." Then here comes my sister Brennan running full speed with a big net and she reached down and netted that big cat. Brennan sure helps me catch a lot of fish.

We took some pictures and that big cat was talking to us the whole time. Mr. Yellow Cat was our friend cause he knew we were going to let him go. I think we catch a lot of fish because they know we are not going to keep them.

I like catching fish a lot more than eating them anyway. I mean if I'm going to eat catfish I'm going to the Bluebonnet Cafe in Marble Falls, Friday night all you can eat. Besides, my Mom said that if we expect her to clean our fish, we better think again. I think what she meant to say was, Bluebonnet Cafe, here we come. I mean, I went to Sunday school, I heard Pastor Doug preach and I caught a monster yellow cat all on the same day. It just doesn't get any better than that.

If you are heading back to the dock with 30 big fish on your stringer and you think the fish need some water, wait until the boat stops before you throw them in. Unless you really don't want to help your dad clean any fish.

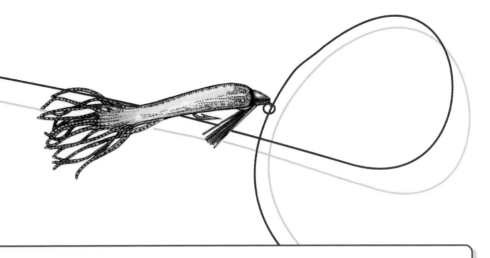

Are we pumped up or what!

"My friend Kallie's first fishing trip and she caught the biggest and wildest fish of the day, a huge Gaftop. I mean that gaftop looks like a catfish with sails."

"Here is my Dad and Uncle Chuck with a huge carp they caught when they were kids."

"Me and Brennan are waiting for the big ones at this kidfish contest. I think all the fish are sleeping."

"Me and Taylor took a break from tubing and caught this nice bass."

"I think Brennan and Caroline are probably going to be Bass'n Gal champions someday."

"Sometimes when the fish aren't biting on the pier all it takes is a little fish dancing to wake em up."

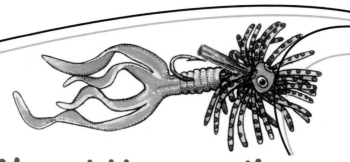

It was Almost Hammertime

One day Dad and Uncle Chuck took me and my cousin Logan fishing in the big ocean. The waves were so big, like a hundred feet tall. We were fishing by some old oil rigs and there was somebody blowing the loudest horn you ever heard on that rig. Dad gave us a seasick pill and I didn't get sick at all. I think it was because I was too sleepy to feel any of those waves.

This day we were trolling and drifting for kingfish, using ribbonfish for bait. A ribbonfish looks like a silver eel with a bunch of teeth. They are some bad looking dudes. Kingfish really like to eat ribbonfish. Once this kingfish wanted to eat my ribbonfish so bad that he swam really fast to eat it and he missed it completely and flew about 50 feet out of the water. I told my Dad, "Now that's a flying fish!" Whenever we hooked one of those big kingfish me and Logan both had to hold onto that rod and Dad would have to hold onto us or we would all get pulled in the ocean. It took us like an hour to bring in one of those big kings. Me and Logan were really tired after catching 10 of those silver flying dudes.

We use huge reels and rods cause in the ocean you might catch a shark or a marlin or even a barracuda. We were about to head back in when we hooked one more big king. It took forever to get this one near the boat. After about thirty minutes we could see that kingfish about twenty feet under the boat and right behind that king was a monster hammerhead shark. That hammerhead was bigger than our boat. It made "Jaws" look like a minnow.

I gave Dad the rod and told him I thought it was probably time for us to head for shore. I didn't want anything to do with that big bad boy. Luckily for us that hammerhead wasn't hungry, he just swam on by. I don't know what I would have done if I would have hooked that dude. Dad said when you hook one of those big baby's......it's Hammertime!!! Fishing in the ocean is awesome cause you never know what you are going to catch, or what is going to catch you!

Always take a camera with you so you can take a picture of your trophy fish before you let it go.

Ankle Deep and Pushing

My first fishing trip to the coast without Mr. Jay was a rough one. I mean the wind was blowing so hard my hat kept blowing off. The waves were huge. Dad said the waves had white caps, whatever that means. This day my friend Taylor and his dad, Mr. Mike, were fishing with us.

Dad had this fishing map that had red circles on it where the fish lived. We fished at every one of those red circles and there were no fish at home. I think somebody must have been tricking us with that map. Mr. Mike said last year somebody tricked him with a map just like ours. After two hours and not even one bite Mr. Mike said, "Should of called Jay." You see, Mr. Jay always knows where the fish are.

Well, Dad was driving the boat to another red circle spot and all of the sudden the boat just stopped, the motor was running, but the boat wasn't moving anymore and land was really far away. Dad stuck his pole in the water and it was not even 6 inches deep. Dad said, "Foster, we found the flats." Dad always tries to make us laugh when something bad happens.

Mr. Mike and my Dad had to get out and push the boat like for a hundred miles. While our Dad's were moaning and groaning and pushing the boat these people in another boat drove by and yelled "When the birds are standing in ankle deep water it usually means it's pretty shallow, you bunch of yee haws." What those guys said made since to me and Taylor. Dad and Mr. Mike, they didn't think it was very funny. They pushed our boat for over an hour. We finally found some deeper water and Dad started the engine and we headed for home. They told us to keep a look out for birds standing in ankle deep water. All the way home Mr. Mike kept saying "Should of called Jay, should of called Jay." Mr. Mike was right ya know.

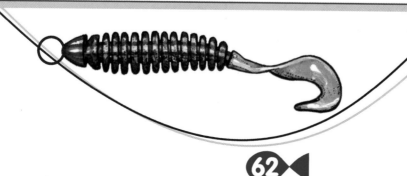

Reel your lures in very slow when the water is really cold. Fish get kind of lazy in cold water.

Big Fishergirls and a Little Fisherboy, Not a Chance

My sisters and I were trolling along our favorite tree line on Lake Travis. We had three poles out, one for each of us. We looked up and Cara's pole was bent half over. I thought she probably hooked a tree. Then this huge bass jumped out of the water and we knew it wasn't a tree. It pulled so hard Cara couldn't even turn her reel. Finally with some help from Dad they reeled that big bass in close enough to the boat for Brennan to net it. It was a monster. Cara was so scared, she didn't even want to hold it for a picture. She was so happy when we finally let that big monster bass go free.

A few minutes later Brennan hooked a fish. It was another huge bass. Brennan fought that bass like a pro and after about 10 minutes she put that trophy in the boat. It was a good 6 pounder. Brennan loves getting her picture taken, so after about a roll of film we finally let it go ,too.

My sisters were catching all the big ones and I couldn't catch even one. I finally hooked a bass and man, it was a baby. My sisters started telling me how they were the big fishergirls and that I was the little fisherboy. I had to catch a big one real soon. It's great if they are the big fishergirls but I am never going to be the little fisherboy.

Dad told me it was time to head in and I begged him to stay a little longer because it wasn't even dark yet. He said I had 10 more minutes. Just when my time was about up I finally hooked a fish. I was just hoping it was not another little one. Oh baby, when that bass jumped I knew the little fisherboy was history. Cara's was still the biggest and Brennan's was even bigger than mine too. But you know what, I'll take a third place five pounder every day I go fishing, especially when my sister's come in first and second.

"Cara's bass was just too big. She didn't like holding it at all."

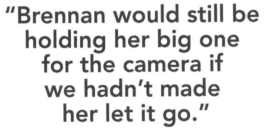

"Brennan would still be holding her big one for the camera if we hadn't made her let it go."

"We were all happy that I finally caught a big one too!"

Foster's Fishing Words

Anchor: This real heavy thing that keeps your boat from floating away. Be sure to tie the rope to your boat before you throw it in the water.

Bait: A bait is anything you use to catch fish. It can be a lure or a live minnow or a squirmy wormy, even a piece of ham will work.

Bay: The calm part of the ocean. Where you catch trout, redfish, flounder and hardheads.

Big Red: A Big Red is a huge fish that we catch in the ocean and in our secret lake. They are kind of red and gold colored with a black spot on their tail. Those reds are some fighting dudes.

Birdsnest: When you cast with a Baitcaster reel and you don't put you thumb on the line before the lure hits the water, all your line will get tangled and make a huge mess that looks just like a bird's nest. Getting birdsnest is just part of fishing with a Baitcaster, everybody gets them. If your dad gets upset with you for getting a birdsnest just asked him if he ever got one.....or a thousand.

Casting: To throw your lure or bait out using your rod and reel. Look out behind you.

Catch and release: This means when you catch a fish you release it and let it go so other kids can have fun catching them.

Cork: A cork is this thing that shoots out of the wine bottle before they spray it everywhere when Jeff or Dale or Mark or Terry or Bobby or one of those Nascar drivers wins the championship. A cork is also a thing that you put on your line that floats. Some corks are round, some are long and skinny, some are big and some are real little, some are red, some are yellow and some are even orange and green. When a fish is playing with your bait the cork will go up and down. Now when a fish eats your bait the cork will go all the way under water and that is when you need to set the hook with a Power Team Pull.

Crankbait: A crankbait is a lure that catches fish when you are reeling it in. Sometimes you crank them slow and sometimes you crank them fast and sometimes you do the stop and go.

Dip Net: This is a big net with a long handle. After you hook a fish and you reel them in you use the net to catch the fish so you don't have to grab them with your hands. Watch out cause some fish have big teeth and bite and some have real sharp fins and all the fish are really slimy.

Downrigger: A downrigger is this thing that looks like a big fishing reel and it makes your lure or bait go really deep in the water.

Early Bite / Late Bite: If the fish are hungry early in the morning, then it is an early bite. If the fish are more hungry later, then it is called a late bite.

Flats: The shallow part of the bay or lake. Where you get your boat stuck.

Getting Spooled: When you hook a fish and they don't like it, they get really mad and take all your line and never look back, that is getting spooled.

Got One, Yeah baby, Bam, There's one, Here we go, Fish on: Things you say when you hook a fish.

Honey Hole: A secret place where you can catch fish everyday.

In the Zone: Being in the zone is when you catch a lot of fish. Like on every cast.

Jerkbait: A jerkbait is a lure that floats and when you jerk it, it goes underwater. When you stop jerking, it goes back to the top. This drives the fish crazy.

Jerk Their Lips Off: What you do to a fish when you set the hook.

Jig and Pig: A jig and pig is a weird bug looking lure that is fished around trees. It's called a jig cause you jig it up and down. The pig is the tail. It doesn't look like a pig, it's called a pig cause it comes from some part of the pig they call pork.

Leader: A leader is some wire or real strong fishing line that goes on the end of your line. You tie one end to your fishing line and the other end to your lure. This makes sure that fish with sharp teeth or fins won't cut your line.

Live bait: Live bait is bait that is alive when you put it on your hook. A bigger fish will then come and eat the bait and then they will get hooked on your line. Live bait is like minnows and perch and croakers and shrimp and grasshoppers and even worms.

Lure: A lure is a fake baby fish or bug that is not real, it just looks real. Most of them are made out of plastic and wood and they have real sharp hooks. When fish get hungry they like to eat the lures. They think they are real food. They eat them, then they get hooked and you reel them in.

Making a Run: This is when you hook a fish and they don't like it, they will swim away like a wild bull, three or four times. Then they will get tired and the victory is yours.

Pier or Dock: A place to fish from. A wood bridge thing that goes from the land out into the water. You can fish from the pier and you can fish under the pier because that is where a lot of fish live. At the lake they have little ones and at the ocean they have huge ones.

Plastic Worm: A plastic worm is a fake worm that feels more like rubber than plastic. You fish these real slow, pulling your pole up and down waiting for a fish to go tap, tap. Worms come in all kinds of shapes and like in a zillion colors.

Practice Plug: A practice plug is like a lure without hooks. You tie it on your line and you practice casting it in your back yard or at the park. Then when you do go fishing you won't catch a bunch of trees, or your dad or other stuff that is not very good.

School of Fish: A school of fish is a bunch of fish playing together, kind of like all the kids in your class playing on the playground.

Set the Hook: When you feel a big fish biting your lure you need to jerk your pole real hard, that is what setting the hook is. This hooks the fish real good so he won't come off. My hook set is called the Power Team Pull.

Shake and Bake: When you hook a big fish and you almost have them in the boat and they make one last jump and shake their head and throw the lure out of their mouth and swim away like a rocket. Well that's the shake and bake and it will make you feel really sick.

Shoot, Darn, Oh Well, What's Up, Dadgum, Oh Man, Can't Believe It, He's Gone: Things you say when you lose a fish.

Smell the Roses: When a fish comes up and eats your topwater lure, he is smelling the roses. That means that lures must smell like roses and I guess fish must like to eat roses. They probably think the hooks are like the thorns. Jay always says, "Foster throw your lure over there and see if those big boys will come up and smell the roses" and they usually do.

Stringer: A piece of little rope that you put your fish on after you catch them so that you can take them home to eat.

The Coast or Beach: This is where the red road runs into the ocean at Port Aransas. There is lots of sand and huge waves. Whatever you do don't drink the water at the beach, man it's salty, and it really burns your eyes too.

The Greatest Fisherman: The best fisherman there ever was and there will ever be is Jesus. I mean he went where they were catching no fish and showed them how to catch so many fish that they couldn't carry them all. He just showed those fishermen that all they needed to have was a little faith.

Tighten the Drag: When you tighten the drag on your reel it makes the line harder to pull out.

Topwater Lure: A topwater lure floats on top of the water. You can pop em, jerk em, buzz em and even swim em. Topwaters are awesome.

Trolling: Trolling is what you do when you have a bunch of kids in the boat who want to fish. You put your lures in the water and then the boat goes real slow and you just hold onto your rod until a fish eats your lure, then you reel them in. Trolling is great cause what kids really like is catching fish, casting and reeling, that's a lot of work. This way you just hold your pole and when you have a fish you bring them in, piece of cake!

Well I guess it's time for me to say goodbye for now. I hope this fishing trip has been as much fun for you as it was for me. You know, I have a great idea. I know a way that we can keep on fishing together for a long, long time. You just send me your favorite fishing pictures and fishing stories and together we can both be part of the next Fishing with Foster adventure book.

By the way, did you hear about my new fan club. It was my little sister Brennan's idea. She said that all of the Nascar drivers and movie stars had fan clubs and that I should have one too. This way we can tell each other about all the fish we catch, how our new secret new lures are working and where the best fishing places are. I'm not charging any of my fishing buddies to be a member so you don't have to pay anything. Just send me a note with your name and address on it and tell me why you like to fish and you're in.

Mail your fishing pictures and fishing stories with your name and address to:

Fishing With Foster

P.O. Box 701790, San Antonio, Texas 78270.

You can also check out all kinds of kool fisherkid stuff on my web page at:

www.fishingwithfoster.com.

For now there are few things us kids need to do.

- If you already fish, don't stop, and take another kid with you the next time you go.
- If you don't fish, get someone to take you now. You are missing way too much fun!
- Always wear your lucky life jacket.
- Put on lots of million proof sunscreen.
- Enjoy the fishing as much as the catching, you're going to be doing a lot more fishing.
- As you grow up tell everyone you see to take care of our rivers and lakes and streams and oceans and all our land and all the animals and all the fish. That way kids like us can keep having fun in the outdoors forever and ever.

FISH ON. . . Foster

World's Greatest Fisherkid's Scrapbook:
A place for your favorite stories, drawings, and photos.

Fishing With Foster Product Ordering Information

Order by Phone:

You can place an order by calling 1-800-603-6041 toll free. You can request information about the Fishing With Foster product line.

Order by Internet:

You can order through the internet by going to my web page at fishingwithfoster.com

Contact us by Postal Mail:

Fishing With Foster
P.O. Box 701790
San Antonio, Texas 78270

Fishing makes me really hungry.

Preston

Hey Farter, You get to fish for Jaws and I get to fish for Nessie.

Jamie from Scotland

My Dad is scared of those little tiny minnows.

Demi

Do cat fish get chased by dog fish?

meow   ruff

Kadie

I caught this catfish that needed a shaver really bad.

Layne

Every time I go fishing the wind blows and blows and blows.

Jacob

You want to know a secret. My Mom caches more fish than my Dad.

JohnDavid

Worms are so YUCKY!!

EMILY

When I go fishing I like to put my toes in the water.

Rachel